GARFIELD

Gotcha!

JIM DAVIS

ℛℛ
RAVETTE PUBLISHING

(www.garfield.com)

First published by Ravette Publishing 2004.

Printed and bound in Great Britain
for Ravette Publishing Limited,
Unit 3, Tristar Centre,
Star Road, Partridge Green,
West Sussex RH13 8RA

by Cox & Wyman, Reading, Berkshire.

ISBN: 1 84161 226 X

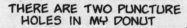

JIM DAVIS 12-20

www.garfield.com

JIM DAVIS 1-2

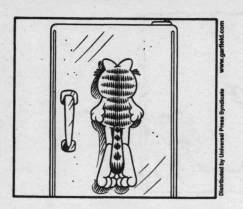

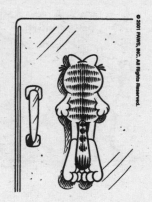

CONGRATULATIONS, YOU HAVE WON THE GRAND PRIZE!

AN EVENING WITH ME

THE EXCITEMENT WAS TOO MUCH

PROBABLY A STOMACH VIRUS

JIM DAVIS 2-9

SOME KIDS HAVE BEEN RINGING OUR DOORBELL AND RUNNING

THIS BUCKET OF WATER WILL TEACH THEM A LESSON!

DING DONG

MY DATE WILL BE HERE ANY SECOND

I DON'T THINK SO

JIM DAVIS 2-24

OTHER GARFIELD BOOKS AVAILABLE

Pocket Books	Price	ISBN
Below Par	£3.50	1 84161 152 2
Bon Appetit	£3.50	1 84161 038 0
Compute This!	£3.50	1 84161 194 8
Double Trouble	£3.50	1 84161 008 9
Eat My Dust	£3.50	1 84161 098 4
Fun in the Sun	£3.50	1 84161 097 6
Goooooal!	£3.50	1 84161 037 2
Great Impressions	£3.50	1 85304 191 2
I Don't Do Perky	£3.50	1 84161 195 6
In Training	£3.50	1 85304 785 6
Light Of My Life	£3.50	1 85304 353 2
On The Right Track	£3.50	1 85304 907 7
Pop Star	£3.50	1 84161 151 4
To Eat, Or Not To Eat?	£3.50	1 85304 991 3
Wave Rebel	£3.50	1 85304 317 6
With Love From Me To You	£3.50	1 85304 392 3

new title now available

No. 49 – S.W.A.L.K.	£3.50	1 84161 225 1

Theme Books		
Guide to Behaving Badly	£4.50	1 85304 892 5
Guide to Cat Napping	£4.50	1 84161 087 9
Guide to Coffee Mornings	£4.50	1 84161 086 0
Guide to Creatures Great & Small	£3.99	1 85304 998 0
Guide to Healthy Living	£3.99	1 85304 972 7
Guide to Pigging Out	£4.50	1 85304 893 3
Guide to Romance	£3.99	1 85304 894 1
Guide to Successful Living	£3.99	1 85304 973 5
Guide to The Seasons	£3.99	1 85304 999 9

new titles now available

Entertains You	£4.50	1 84161 221 9
Slam Dunk!	£4.50	1 84161 222 7

2-in-1 Theme Books		
Easy Does It	£6.99	1 84161 191 3
Licensed to Thrill	£6.99	1 84161 192 1
Out For The Couch	£6.99	1 84161 144 1
The Gruesome Twosome	£6.99	1 84161 143 3

new titles now available

All in Good Taste	£6.99	1 84161 209 X
Lazy Daze	£6.99	1 84161 208 1

Classics	Price	ISBN
Volume One	£5.99	1 85304 970 0
Volume Two	£5.99	1 85304 971 9
Volume Three	£5.99	1 85304 996 4
Volume Four	£5.99	1 85304 997 2
Volume Five	£5.99	1 84161 022 4
Volume Six	£5.99	1 84161 023 2
Volume Seven	£5.99	1 84161 088 7
Volume Eight	£5.99	1 84161 089 5
Volume Nine	£5.99	1 84161 149 2
Volume Ten	£5.99	1 84161 150 6
Volume Eleven	£5.99	1 84161 175 1
Volume Twelve	£5.99	1 84161 176 X

new titles now available

Volume Thirteen	£5.99	1 84161 206 5
Volume Fourteen	£5.99	1 84161 207 3

Little Books		
C-c-c-caffeine	£2.50	1 84161 183 2
Food 'n' Fitness	£2.50	1 84161 145 X
Laughs	£2.50	1 84161 146 8
Love 'n' Stuff	£2.50	1 84161 147 6
Surf 'n' Sun	£2.50	1 84161 186 7
The Office	£2.50	1 84161 184 0
Wit 'n' Wisdom	£2.50	1 84161 148 4
Zzzzzzz	£2.50	1 84161 185 9

Miscellaneous		
Garfield the Movie	£7.99	1 84161 205 7
Garfield 25 years of me!	£7.99	1 84161 173 5
Treasury 4	£10.99	1 84161 180 8
Treasury 3	£9.99	1 84161 142 5

new title now available

Treasury 5	£10.99	1 84161 198 0

All Garfield books are available at your local bookshop or from the publisher at the address below. Just tick the titles required and send the form with your payment to:-

RAVETTE PUBLISHING
Unit 3, Tristar Centre, Star Road, Partridge Green, West Sussex RH13 8RA

Prices and availability are subject to change without notice.
Please enclose a cheque or postal order made payable to **Ravette Publishing** to the value of the cover price of the book and allow the following for UK postage and packing:

60p for the first book + 30p for each additional book
except *Garfield Treasuries* when please add £3.00 per copy for p&p

Name ....

Address ....

....

....